★ ★ ★ ★ ★

How To Be A Good President

Lessons from Kids

★

 Each lesson includes *Action Steps for Kids*

GROWN-UPS, PARENTS & TEACHERS:
Additional information to help teach these lessons
can be found in the white boxes.

ATTENTION SCHOOLS & ORGANIZATIONS:
A portion of our proceeds goes toward putting free books in kids' hands.
We'll send free copies to your school, club, or community.
FOR DETAILS, CONTACT INFO@WYATTMACKENZIE.COM WITH YOUR REQUEST.

Text and Illustrations © 2017 Wyatt-MacKenzie Publishing.
All rights reserved.

ISBN: 978-1-942545-85-9
For large quantity orders contact info@wyattmackenzie.com.

This is a work of fiction.
The characters and events in this book are fictitious.
Any similarity to any real person is coincidental.

Wyatt-MacKenzie Publishing
DEADWOOD, OREGON

There is no implied endorsement of this book by authors, illustrators, editors, proofreaders, or reviewers
of the previous projects which inspired it. The publisher wishes to thank everyone who persists.

Dear President,

You're the most important person in the country! Kids are counting on you, and we want to help.

We want to share the lessons we learned—when we were little—to help you be a good president.

Please enjoy *How To Be A Good President*. It has our best advice and action steps for kids to follow … straight to the White House!

~ Kids of America

Action Steps for Kids

★ Share a toy or treat.

★ Let a friend choose what game to play or which toy to play with.

★ Remember a lesson that your parents or teachers taught you and put it into practice at the next opportunity.

★ Do an act of kindness, without being asked, or asking to be recognized.

★ Don't lecture a friend, instead show them how to behave.

★ Treat peers fairly and do not gossip.

Actions speak louder than words. How we behave sends a powerful message about what we believe. Children often are instructed to do what they are told and not question it (following the old adage, "do as I say, not as I do"), but every parent knows that children learn more from what they *see* their parents and other authorities do, than from the more abstract rules and lessons passed along to them.

Lesson #1
Actions Speak Louder than Words

Kids know that what we *do* matters
more than what we *say*.
This is an important lesson in leadership.

Action Steps for Kids

★ Be friendly to everyone.

★ Follow good examples, and avoid examples of behavior you know are wrong even if it's a friend you see doing them.

★ Try to persuade a friend to be kind and to compromise.

★ Avoid saying negative things even to people who are not being nice.

★ Invite new people to play with you and your friends.

★ Don't give in to peer pressure to do or say something you know is wrong.

★ Don't abandon a friend just because others don't like him or her.

★ Talk to a friend and be honest if they are starting to behave in ways that make you uncomfortable.

Choose your friends wisely. Friends quickly become some of the most influential people in a child's life, and in their development. When we teach them to choose their friends wisely, parents are acknowledging the importance of these potentially life-long relationships. We are also urging our children to recognize the influence their friends have on them and the impact they can have in return. It is an important responsibility that should not be taken lightly. Just as when America chooses allies in the world speaks volumes about what kind of nation we are, children need to realize that how their friends act also says a great deal about them.

Lesson #2
Choose Your Friends Wisely

Kids act like the crowd we hang out with
(and so do world leaders).
We should find friends who set a good example.

Action Steps for Kids

★ Clean up your toys, your room, and any mess you make.

★ Treat places you visit with respect and leave them cleaner than you found them.

★ Conserve energy: turn off your lights, TV, and other electronics, and shut doors.

★ Clean up messes that others have made; after all, someone has to take care of the planet!

★ Ask your parents if your family can create a "family plan" to reduce energy consumption in your household.

★ Recycle! Use recyclable materials whenever possible – be creative.

★ Go through your toys and clothes in the spring and fall – give away, don't throw away!

★ Ask your teachers to consider a school program to exchange ideas within your school or with another school about taking better care of the planet.

★ Be responsible for your actions by replacing or fixing things you have accidentally broken or damaged.

★ Volunteer for clean-up events in your community.

Clean up your own mess. This lesson has two meanings. The first is straight-forward but critical to the health of our environment. Cleaning up our messes and being earth-friendly is going to be even more important for our kids, and their kids, than it was for us. The other meaning is more subtle, but equally important. When children show accountability for their actions, they demonstrate their understanding that what they do can have a wide-ranging impact. The best leaders understand this concept and live by it.

Lesson #3
Clean Up Your Own Mess

As kids take responsibility for ourselves,
we make the world a better place for all.

Action Steps for Kids

★ Walk away from a bully or don't respond to their verbal or online teasing.

★ Often bullying can start with a misunderstanding, which can be fixed when people talk to each other respectfully.

★ Don't abandon a true friend if they are being picked on. Help them find an adult who can help.

★ Talk to someone you think might be angry with you, and see if they just don't understand something, or if they're afraid. Sometimes peers act in a mean way when they really just want to be friends.

★ Help friends, who are not getting along with each other, to compromise and become friends again!

Don't give in to a bully. Don't give in to a bully. Bullies feed on fear. Ignoring a bully is the hardest thing to do and requires a lot more courage than responding to their taunts. Standing up to any kind of bullying requires self-esteem. When children take this lesson into adulthood, they will have learned to be true to themselves, and their beliefs, regardless of who challenges them. When they apply this lesson as citizens, they will ensure that America does not abandon its ideals when it is threatened. Each bullying situation requires careful understanding of the root causes of the problem. Above all, children should know they can turn to adults for help.

Lesson #4
Don't Give in to a Bully

When kids have the courage to resist bullying,
we show others how to stand up to fear.

Action Steps for Kids

★ If something bad happens, tell the truth about what you did immediately. You'll be amazed how telling the truth can become a good habit. Adults will praise you for being brave. You may still get punished, but you'll feel a lot better about yourself for being honest.

★ Don't argue when you know you are wrong.

★ Admit the truth before anyone asks you and even if you "got away with it."

★ Tell the whole truth, not just the part you are asked about.

★ If your friends are considering doing something wrong, discuss the downside and don't give in to peer pressure. Chances are that your friends may also thinking about the negative consequences, but are afraid to say something.

★ Offer to make amends if you've done something wrong. Admitting the truth is the first step. The next step is trying to make up for what you've done, which is truly admirable.

Tell the truth. Telling the truth sounds a lot easier than it is. Sometimes kids are only asked to tell part of the truth and it's much easier to withhold the rest. Other times, they may "get away with" doing something wrong and they don't see the point of confessing. But telling the truth, the whole truth, no matter how difficult the consequences, will be certain to earn them respect.

Lesson #5
Tell the Truth

When kids tell the truth we will be well-respected,
which is the key to being a good leader.

Action Steps for Kids

★ Take turns.

★ Be respectful in your class, team, or club by listening to instructors and peers.

★ Volunteer your time or talent to a local cause.

★ Start a club or volunteer activity. Look for a need that is not being filled in your school, neighborhood, or community. It could be as simple as offering to take a meal to an elderly or sick neighbor.

★ Run for office in your school – be a member of your student council.

★ Keep up with local news – ask your parents or teachers for good sources of information. Watch political debates at election time and get to know the candidates. **Informed voters are the best voters!**

Participate! Anyone can be a leader. Leadership starts with participation. Participation starts with using one's voice and volunteering to help. Children can begin with something small, and they might be surprised at how much impact they have. When children learn the power of participation in their community, they are learning how to be responsible citizens and eventually great leaders.

Lesson #6
Participate!

When kids get involved in our communities and help others, we are being good citizens, and would make good presidents someday!

Thank you for reading!

Now it's your turn. Add your own ideas to these pages. Write **Lesson #7** and create a drawing. Then come up with your own action steps and list them here!

Action Steps for Kids

★ _____
  _____.

★ _____
  _____.

★ _____
  _____.

★ _____
  _____.

★ _____
  _____.

Lesson #7